Australia's
Meteorite Craters

Alex Bevan and Ken McNamara

Foreword by Robert Hough

GOVERNMENT OF
WESTERN AUSTRALIA

WESTERN AUSTRALIAN
muSEum

Contents

Left: Time lapse star trails around the south celestial pole above Wolfe Creek Crater *(photo John Goldsmith / Celestial Visions)*.

Foreword

One look at the pitted surface of the Moon shows the effects of impact cratering in the past. The spectacular images of the fragmented comet Shoemaker-Levy 9 crashing into Jupiter in 1994, and more recently another event on Jupiter in July 2009, show us that collisions between bodies in the Solar System continue today. On Earth, unlike the Moon, we have plate tectonics, erosion and deposition of new sediments, and much of our surface is covered in oceans. This makes finding ancient craters very difficult. Nonetheless, the deeply eroded remnants of impact craters up to 300 kilometres in diameter have been found, and some are as old as two billion years. Others are concealed beneath much younger rocks. Large craters are rare, but smaller ones are more common. What we call small craters might still be five kilometres across, and the small asteroids that formed them would have been about 500 metres wide and travelling at about 55,000 kilometres/hour!

All the rock excavated from the crater would have been pulverised, heated and thrown outwards, or raised in a giant plume to herald the catastrophe. Some material may have been jetted out as melted droplets to land as tektites great distances from the impact site. If you sit in the tranquil surroundings of the 0.9-kilometre Wolfe Creek Crater (a tourist attraction in Western Australia) trying to imagine its violent beginnings, remember that there are impact structures up to a thousand times bigger than Wolfe Creek Crater on Earth.

Over the past fifty years many circular structures that were once thought to be volcanic have now been shown to have an impact (meteorite, comet or asteroid) origin. Today we know that many impacts, like Sudbury in Canada, are associated with economic mineral deposits. Others like Chicxulub in Mexico have been linked to biological extinctions. Australia has thirty-seven of these scars, ranging in size from a few metres to tens of kilometres across, and there are many other suspects under investigation. Once the unique, telltale evidence of high pressures and temperatures are found in the surrounding rocks or in the structure itself, then the 'suspect' can be added to the global list of confirmed impact craters that currently number about 176. If the impact is small, producing a crater only a few hundreds of metres or less across, then fragments of the meteorite will often survive. In larger impacts the projectile is completely melted and vaporised. The ancient and large land surface of Australia is a window into Earth's past, revealing the remarkable history of bombardment it has endured. Continued exploration in Australia for hidden oil and mineral wealth will undoubtedly reveal more of the now concealed record. New circular features seen from the air or by satellites may turn out to be impact craters. Often it is not the cratering expert that discovers these craters but geologists and prospectors going about their daily business. Each newly discovered crater is unique in some way and provides a new and exciting insight into their formation, which is important if we are to understand the role craters have played in the physical, biological, environmental and economic evolution of Earth.

Robert Hough
Exploration and Mining, CSIRO, Perth, Western Australia

Above: Wolfe Creek Crater (*photo Dainis Dravins, Lund Observatory, Sweden*).

Preface

The deep craters on the Moon are the scars from intense bombardment by debris from the Solar System more than 3,900 million years ago. On Earth, although younger meteorite impact craters are known, slow but relentless geological forces have combined to wipe the record of this early event from its surface. In that same 3,900 million years on Earth, continents have risen, seas and oceans have opened and closed, mountains have been raised and ground down to their roots again by the action of wind and water, volcanoes have poured molten lava from Earth's hot interior ... and life has evolved. Nevertheless, around 176 younger structures of authenticated or probable meteorite impact origin have been recognised worldwide, and recently there has been an upsurge of interest in the role that giant impacts may have played in the evolution of the Solar System and of Earth itself. The surviving impact structures provide the only tangible evidence against which theoretical predictions of the effects of potentially catastrophic impact can be compared. Amongst other hypotheses, researchers have linked colossal asteroidal impact with the formation of Earth's early ocean basins and the Moon itself, as well as mass biological extinctions in the geological past. How are craters formed? How often have catastrophic impacts occurred on Earth, and what effects have they had? Most importantly, can they happen again and do they pose a threat to civilisation? Using Wolfe Creek Crater and other Australian examples, this book examines the role of meteorite impact as a significant geological process that has helped to shape our planet.

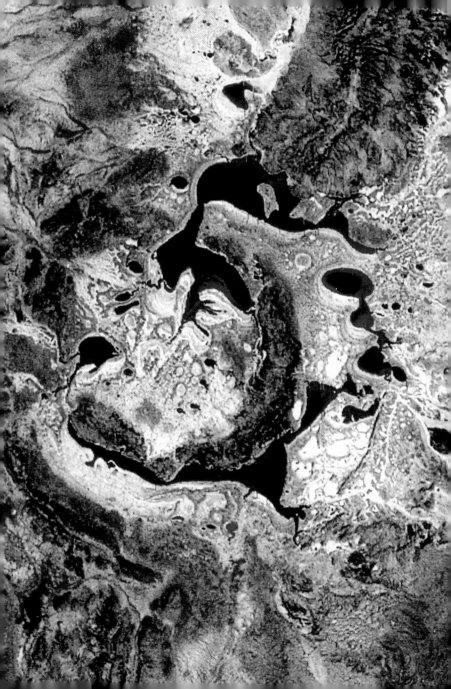

Introduction

Australia is an ancient land. Some of the rocks in the Pilbara region of Western Australia, for instance, are 3,500 million years old, while some sedimentary rocks from Mt Narryer have been dated at around 3,000 million years and contain much older mineral grains derived from pre-existing rocks that are 4,400 million years old. Earth itself is about 4,560 million years old. Many of the rocks that make up the core of the continent are also thousands of millions of years old. Some of these ancient rocks have lain undisturbed for almost 1,000 million years, while other rocks twice this age represent the roots of great mountain chains that once towered high into Earth's young atmosphere. This was long before the land was clothed with vegetation and animals had emerged from the seas onto the land.

Left: Viewed from space, the giant Shoemaker (thirty kilometres in diameter) structure (formerly known as Teague Ring) at the eastern edge of the Frere Range in Western Australia is thought to be around 600 million years old (*photo Landgate, Western Australia, and the Australian Centre for Remote Sensing [ACRES]*).

Rain falling onto bare hills carved channels; the Sun blazed on the rocks; the winds howled across the barren land. For hundreds of millions of years the Sun, wind and rain plucked the sand grains from rocks and wore mountain chains down to their roots. Today rivers still wind fitfully over these ancient, eroded mountain chains, while in other areas the wind shifts the sand derived from these worn-down mountains in the great dune fields that march across the now arid wastes.

The Australian landscape, then, has been gradually transformed by the agencies of weathering, which still continue at a gentle pace. But a few features scattered over the land seem to defy any explanation of formation by Earth's normal slow weathering and geological processes. The sculptured landscape of hills and valleys is occasionally pitted by regular circular structures, often no more than faintly hinting at their existence. At other times they are clearly recognisable as large, deep craters.

In Australia seven distinct craters, ranging in size from about twenty-five metres to around one kilometre in diameter, have been recognised. Five

Above: Aerial view of Wolfe Creek Crater from the northwest. The crater occupies Bulara District Location 16 and was first gazetted as a Class C Reserve in 1969. In 1976 the crater was made a Class A Reserve (No 29457) and is now controlled and managed by the Department of Environment and Conservation (DEC) in Western Australia (*photo the Australian News and Information Bureau*).

of these are associated with meteorites. In addition, there are another thirty very much larger but deeply eroded and enigmatic circular scars that present some evidence of an origin by impact. Among the largest are Woodleigh in Western Australia, Lake Acraman in South Australia and Tookoonooka in Queensland, which are probably 60–70 kilometres, greater than 35 kilometres, and 50 kilometres in diameter respectively. While their diameters have yet to be determined precisely, these three structures are clearly very old, and in the case of Woodleigh and Tookoonooka they have become buried beneath

Above: Geologists examine Dalgaranga crater north of Yalgoo in Western Australia (*photo V Humphrey*).

a mantle of younger sediments, such that they are no longer visible at the surface.

Twelve other structures have been recognised, either as surface features or by geophysics. For these there is little or no evidence other than their circularity to prove they are of impact origin. These structures include one submarine structure, Maningrida, which occurs off the coast of northern Australia. On land, eleven structures tentatively identified as possible impact sites include Lorne Basin (a doubtful structure in New South Wales); Gnargoo, Herbert, Ilkura, Lennis, and Skirmish (all in Western Australia); Mingobar (Queensland); and Barramundi, Calvert Hills, Renehan and Wessel (all in the Northern Territory). At this stage the origin of

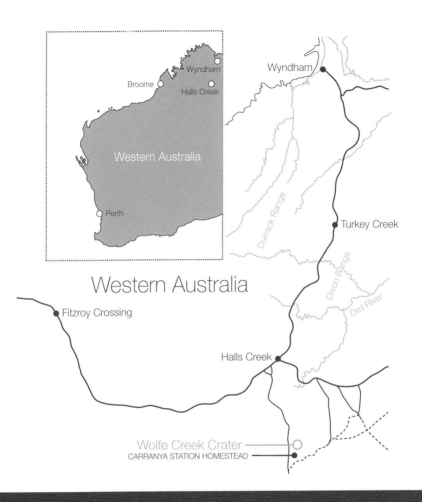

Western Australia

Wolfe Creek Crater is reasonably accessible, lying close to the Halls Creek-Balgo Community road, seven kilometres north of Carranya Station. The unsealed road from Halls Creek is generally open from May to October. It is usually impassable between January and April. It is recommended that advice on road condition be sought from the Shire Clerk at Halls Creek.

these anomalies, both on land and in the sea, are considered speculative. In total then, some forty-nine structures have been recognised in Australia to highly varying degrees of certainty, ranging from authenticated to doubtful.

The question is, how did these craters and circular structures form? It is clear that most were formed by explosions. But was the source of the explosions from within Earth's crust, or was it an extraterrestrial source, such as a giant meteorite, asteroid or comet hitting Earth?

Of all the craters in Australia, Wolfe Creek Crater is the most spectacular visually and one of the best studied. Unfortunately, ideas on the origin of the crater, one of the most fascinating structures in Australia, languish in learned scientific journals. In this book, using Wolfe Creek Crater as a classic example we examine how this crater and the other recognised structures formed, and perhaps show how scientists must often act as sleuths, carefully scrutinising all the evidence for clues to track down their origins.

Right: Satellite image of Wolfe Creek Crater (*photo NASA's Earth Observatory*).

Discovery
and Ancient Beliefs

Travelling south from Halls Creek, the hilly country of the southeastern Kimberley quickly gives way to the flat sand plains of the northeastern Great Sandy Desert. Some ninety kilometres south of Halls Creek and a little to the east of Wolfe Creek, we see on the horizon a break in the monotonous flat spinifex sand plain: an apparently flat-topped hill. In these endless plains it is hard to judge the height and distance of the hill, but after another ten kilometres we are almost there.

The fascinating story of the Wolfe Creek Crater begins to be revealed as we approach the slopes of the hill where the quartzite country rock becomes increasingly broken and disarranged. Areas of laterite, which cap the quartzite, become

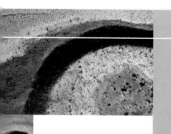

factf(ocu)s

Historical note: Originally named 'Wolf Creek'; historical research revealed that the person after whom the locality is named was called 'Wolfe' and the locality has been accordingly renamed Wolfe Creek.

increasingly fragmented. Then curious objects begin to appear. Close to the top of the hill, on its western slopes, rusty balls of rock lie scattered on the ground, sometimes fused into the laterite and at other times lying loose.

Reaching the top of the hill we gasp from something other than shortness of breath, for before us lies one of the most startling geological features in Australia: Wolfe Creek Crater.

Wolf Creek Crater situated at latitude 19° 10'S., longitude 127° 48'E is almost perfectly circular, its diameter varying between 870 and 950 metres.

This is also how local Aborigines would have first come across the crater long ago. The crater is known to the local Djaru tribe, who call it Kandimalal. Their mythology speaks of two rainbow snakes whose sinuous paths across the desert formed the nearby Sturt Creek and Wolfe Creek. The crater represents the place where one of the snakes emerged from the ground. It was not until as recently as 1947, however, that the crater was first recognised by

Europeans; it was observed from the air by F Reeves, NB Sauve and D Hart during an aerial survey of the Canning Basin. Two months later Reeves and Hart, with H Evans, visited the crater on the ground and made a detailed investigation of the structure. Since that time it has been visited by many scientists from around the world and has also become a popular tourist attraction.

Right: Aerial view of Wolfe Creek Crater from the east (*photo the Australian News and Information Bureau).*

Anatomy
of a Crater

Above: Looking down into Wolfe Creek Crater from the rim.

Wolfe Creek Crater, situated at latitude 19°10'S, longitude 127°48'E, is almost perfectly circular, its diameter varying between 870 and 950 metres. The outer slopes of the crater rise up at an angle of about fifteen degrees to form a ridge, which may be up to thirty-five metres above the surrounding sand plain, ringing the crater. The inner walls plunge more steeply at angles of as much as forty degrees and form cliffs to the flat crater floor some fifty-five metres below the rim. The crater floor has a diameter of about 675 metres and lies as much as twenty-five metres below the level of the surrounding plain. Originally it would have been much deeper, maybe even 120 metres deep, but it is now largely filled with sand.

The crater is partially mantled by sand dunes that lie up against the eastern side of the crater. Two arms of dunes then extend westward. The crater is clearly forming a barrier to dune movement from east to west, as the area directly west of the crater is quite clear of dunes.

The inner walls of the crater expose the quartzite country rock in which the crater is formed. The quartzite is probably of Devonian age, more than 360 million years old. In the area around the crater the quartzite is flat-bedded, but in the walls of the

factf(ocu)s

At twenty-four metres in diameter, Dalgaranga (discovered in 1921 but only recognised in 1923) is one of the smallest meteorite impact craters known, and the earliest recognised in Australia.

crater it is variably deformed and bent. On the eastern wall the rocks dip at about twenty degrees, whereas in the southwest and northwest parts the dip is very steep and the beds of rocks are turned over on themselves. Laterite sandwiched between the layers of folded quartzite in these areas indicates overturning of the beds during formation of the crater.

The current floor of the crater is generally flat. It is largely sand covered and, depending on seasonal variations, supports a sparse growth of spinifex and scattered trees. The central area, made of porous gypsum, supports the densest vegetation and is pierced by a number of sinkholes. Trees of an unusually large size for the area grow here, no doubt drawing on reserves of water trapped after summer rains. The sinkholes lie along two intersecting lines and probably reflect the position of underlying stress fractures formed by

If a large meteorite plummeted to Earth and excavated the crater on impact, then where are most of the remains of the meteorite?

Above: A. Shale-ball from the rim of Wolfe Creek Crater (*photo R Hudson*). B. Impact melt glasses splashed from the crater during its formation (*photo K. Brimmell*).

the explosive excavation of the crater.

The outer slopes of the crater are covered by many broken quartzite slabs and remnants of the laterite veneer that covered much of the land surface before the crater was formed. An intriguing aspect of the outer slopes of the crater is the occurrence of what have been called 'shale-balls' — largely rounded objects made predominantly of iron oxide that are often tapered at one end. Specimens, including some weighing as much as 250 kilograms, occur mainly on these outer slopes, though small shale-balls occur rarely within the crater. Sometimes these shale-balls occur in clusters, and often they are actually welded to the surface of the laterite. Some shale-balls have yielded two minerals previously unknown to science: reevesite, a nickel-iron carbonate; and cassidyite, a calcium-nickel-magnesium phosphate. These rare nickel-bearing minerals provide us with an important clue to the origin of the shale-balls, and the crater itself.

Right: Discovered in July 1975 and subsequently named after an Australian geologist, Veevers Crater (seventy metres in diameter) is situated between the Great Sandy and Gibson Deserts in Western Australia and is one of the best-preserved craters of its size in the world *(photo AN Yeates, Geoscience Australia)*.

A Meteoritic Fingerprint

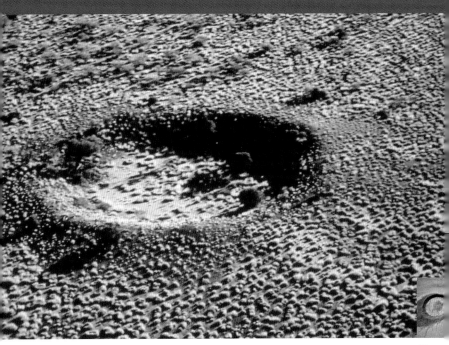

At Wolfe Creek iron meteorites have been found in the neighbourhood of the crater, although in small numbers. In 1965 P Kolbe and E Pederson found 1,343 grams of iron meteorites 3.9 kilometres southwest of the crater in an elliptical area thirty by twenty metres. The largest piece weighed 72.6 grams and, like the other pieces, was an angular fragment, part of a larger body that had broken up. The fragments consist mainly of iron, apart from 8.6% nickel and 0.4–0.5% cobalt.

What, then, are the curious shale-balls that litter the crater slopes? We know that very similar objects occur at many other large craters in other parts of the world and they, likewise, are made predominantly of iron oxides. A close examination of many shale-

In Australia five craters (Boxhole, Dalgaranga, Henbury, Veevers and Wolfe Creek Crater) are associated with remnant meteorite fragments that prove their origin by impact.

Above: Aerial view of Wolfe Creek Meteorite Crater, viewed from the east, looking towards the centre of the crater *(photo John Goldsmith / Celestial Visions)*.

balls at Wolfe Creek has shown that they contain rare fragments and veins of unweathered iron-nickel metal, and grains of the iron-nickel phosphide mineral schreibersite, a characteristic accessory mineral in many iron meteorites. The conclusion is that the shale-balls represent the deeply rusted remains of iron meteorites. The nickel minerals reevesite and cassidyite, and a nickel silicate mineral pecoraite, that occur in the shale-balls were produced by alteration during weathering and are also suggestive of a meteoritic origin for these objects.

Why then do the shale-balls only occur in the vicinity of the crater? To understand this we need to examine in more detail how the crater was formed.

Right: Wolfe Creek Crater *(photo Dainis Dravins, Lund Observatory, Sweden)*

How was Wolfe Creek Crater Formed?

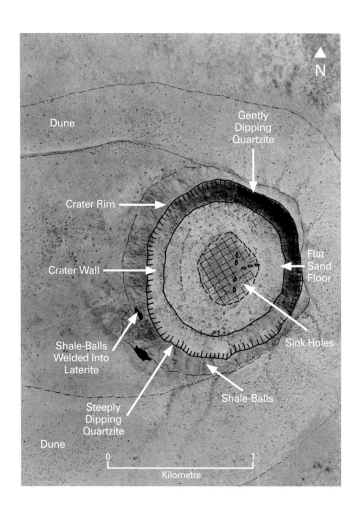

Above: Plan view of Wolfe Creek Crater illustrating principal features.

Wolfe Creek Crater is one of eighteen craters known around the world, both on the land and in the oceans, that are associated with meteorites (including the famous Canyon Diablo, Meteor, or Barringer Crater in Arizona; and the Henbury Craters in central Australia). These large, enigmatic craters were obviously formed by violent explosions, and the occurrence of meteorites in their vicinity is powerful evidence that they were formed by the impact of large meteorites striking Earth.

During the formation of Wolfe Creek Crater, a large volume of rock clearly disappeared; it was either pulverised and dispersed as a dust cloud, or vaporised. A little of this rock is apparent around the crater in the form of single blocks weighing many tonnes that have been thrown out onto the rim. The variable deformation of the quartzite in the crater walls suggests that if indeed a meteoritic projectile caused the explosion, it travelled from the northeast to the southwest. This can be deduced from the greater proportion of fractured rock piled up in the southwestern part of the crater, and it is here that the rocks have been most strongly folded. Further

Stages in the formation of a simple impact crater

1 Small meteoroids are slowed by friction in the atmosphere and fall harmlessly onto Earth as meteorites. Meteoroids weighing hundreds of tonnes are more massive than the column of air beneath them and are not slowed.

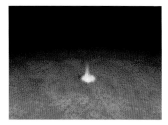

2 In crater-forming impacts, the fireball caused by the high-speed travel of the meteoroid through the atmosphere continues to Earth's surface. These cosmic missiles retain most of their original speed, which is greater than 11.2 kms per second — around forty times faster than a bullet from a high-powered rifle.

3 Immediately on impact the meteorite is rapidly slowed but can still move at around five kilometres per second into the ground. The final depth of penetration depends on the size of the meteorite, its speed and angle, and the nature of the target rocks.

4 The impacting body buries itself deep inside the earth. As it is flattened by compression, the meteorite shatters, melts the country rocks ahead of it and is stopped almost instantaneously. The colossal energy the meteorite has because of its mass and speed is converted to heat and it melts and vaporises.

5 Underground, a huge opening forms and a shock wave expands rapidly away from the point of impact. As the cavity expands, melted rock and projectile material are shot out behind the shock front.

6 A shell of pulverised and melted country rock and meteorite material forms around the cavity. At this point the shock wave is reflected back blasting upwards and outwards in every direction.

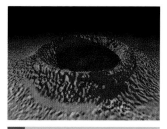

7 The surrounding rock is uplifted and overturned as material behind the reflected shock wave is thrown out of the crater.

8 Fragments thrown out of the crater fall back to build layers of rubble around the crater in the reverse order to that which they were excavated. The walls of the crater slump back towards the centre of the crater.

evidence of the direction of the projectile lies in the distribution of the shale-balls and meteorite fragments. Both are mainly found southwest of the crater: the shale-balls on the outer crater slopes, and the fresh meteorites nearly four kilometres away.

If a large meteorite plummeted to Earth and excavated the crater on impact, then where are most of the remains of the meteorite? Are they buried beneath the crater? Intuitively, we would expect to find lots of pieces of the meteorite both inside and around the crater. Why are there no meteorites to be found inside the crater? The answers to these questions lie in an understanding of the dynamics of meteorite impact.

Small meteorites are slowed by friction in the atmosphere, and neither the meteorites nor the ground on which they fall suffer much damage. Large bodies weighing hundreds or thousands of tonnes are more massive than the column of air they displace and are not slowed appreciably by friction in the atmosphere. These colossal projectiles retain a substantial proportion of their initial, 'cosmic' velocity and hit Earth at speeds in excess of fifteen kilometres/second (rather like crossing Australia in less than five minutes!). The release of immense stored energy on impact would cause an explosion exceeding that of the most powerful nuclear bomb.

One of the world's best known and extensively studied examples of a meteorite explosion crater is Meteor, or Barringer, Crater in Arizona, USA. The bowl-shaped crater, measuring 1.2 kilometres in diameter and 170 metres deep, was formed about fifty thousand years ago by the explosive impact of a mass of meteoritic iron estimated to have weighed more than 100,000 tonnes. In 1927 an enterprising engineering company drilled exploratory shafts in the crater floor to locate and mine the large metallic 'asteroid' they believed to be buried beneath the

factf(o)cus

In crater forming impacts, the fireball caused by high speed flight of the projectile through the atmosphere continues to the ground. These cosmic missiles retain most of their original speed which is greater than 11.2 kilometres per second.

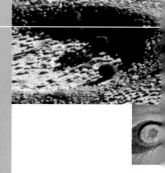

crater. At that time, the way in which meteorite explosion craters form was poorly understood. Basic scientific research revealed the futility of the venture.

When a massive meteorite travelling at high velocity collides with Earth, the object punches a hole, pulverising the rocks deep below the surface. In a fraction of a second, the projectile is stopped and the immense energy generated as a result of its enormous mass and velocity is instantaneously converted to heat. Consequently the projectile itself, and a portion of the surrounding country rock, is melted and vaporised and the attendant shock waves blast away the overburden, jetting debris upwards and outwards in every direction. Upturned strata and a rim raised above the surrounding country, splendidly exhibited at Meteor Crater and Wolfe Creek, are characteristic features of meteorite explosion craters. As the result of the formation of an explosion crater, the bulk of the meteorite is destroyed. This sets an upper limit (approximately 100 tonnes) on the size of meteorites expected to survive as single bodies, and for dynamic reasons meteorites are rarely found within explosion craters.

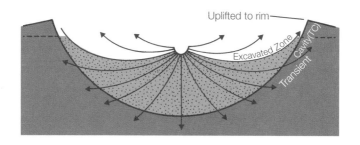

Uplifted to rim
Excavated Zone
Transient Cavity (TC)

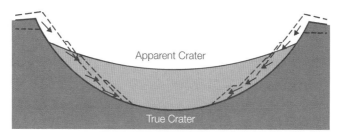

Apparent Crater
True Crater

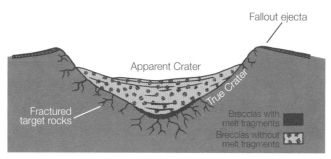

Fallout ejecta
Apparent Crater
True Crater
Fractured target rocks
Breccias with melt fragments
Breccias without melt fragments

Above: Schematic cross-section of a simple crater (bottom), with the stages in the formation of the crater cavity shown above (after Grieve, 1987).

Following Page: Wolfe Creek Crater (*photo Fugro*).

Wolfe Creek Crater formed around 300,000 years ago. On the eastern side, the crater rim is partially obscured by sand dunes. At the time of formation the crater would have been much deeper, but it is now largely filled with wind-blown sand.

At Meteor Crater, as testimony to the origin of the crater more than thirty tonnes of meteoritic iron have been recovered from the rim of the crater and the surrounding plain. Those found on the rim of the crater are twisted and deformed, shrapnel-like fragments.

After Meteor Crater, Wolfe Creek Crater is the second largest authenticated meteorite crater associated with meteorites on land in the world. Several larger structures that are also associated with meteorites are known at Rio Cuarto in Argentina, but their origin by meteorite impact is currently disputed. The largest known structure associated with meteorites lies beneath the ocean between South America and Antarctica, at Eltanin in the Bellingshausen Sea. Wolfe Creek Crater is older and more deeply weathered than Meteor Crater. Sophisticated dating techniques carried out on remnants of the impacting meteorite and the country rocks of the crater show that Wolfe Creek Crater was formed around 300,000 years ago.

Right: The deeply eroded Spider impact structure (eleven by thirteen kilometres) in the Kimberley of Western Australia. The curious sinuous hills and valleys are the erosional remnants of thrusting in the target rocks caused by low-angle impact (photo BHP Minerals).

Australia's Impact Record

Above: Satellite image of Wolfe Creek Crater (*photo ACRES*)

Five craters associated with meteorites occur in Australia, of which three are in Western Australia: Wolfe Creek Crater, Dalgaranga (twenty-four metres in diameter), north of Yalgoo and Veevers Crater (seventy metres in diameter), situated between the Great Sandy and Gibson Deserts. The other structures are Henbury (a group of thirteen craters, the largest measuring 180 metres in diameter), and Boxhole (170 metres in diameter), both of which are in the Northern Territory. There are additional craters at Mount Darwin (Darwin Crater, one kilometre in diameter) in Tasmania, and Hickman (260 metres in diameter) in Western Australia, but while these craters are most probably of meteorite impact origin no meteorites have been found in their vicinity.

Above: Crater map of Australia (see text and the table on page 82–83 for further details).

factf⦿cus

Globally, 176 circular scars have been recognised with certainty as of impact origin. Thirty of these occur in Australia. Another seven structures have been recognised in Australia, but so far lack conclusive proof, while a further twelve enigmatic features are under investigation.

Wolfe Creek Crater, Henbury, Boxhole, Veevers, Dalgaranga, Darwin Crater and Hickman are all 'simple' structures. So-called simple structures form from impacting projectiles that are generally less than a few tens of metres in diameter and produce bowl-shaped craters with raised rims. In the formation of a simple crater, the impact generates a shock wave and a release wave. These waves compress, melt, vaporise and excavate the target rocks, creating a cavity. Eventually the cavity wall collapses inward, leaving a lense of brecciated rock surrounded by highly fractured target rocks.

At diameters above about two kilometres in sedimentary rocks and around four kilometres in harder, crystalline rocks, impact structures take on a more complex form. Splendid examples are the colossal 30-kilometre-diameter Shoemaker structure (formerly known as Teague Ring) that punctuates the Frere Range in central Western Australia, and the famous Gosses Bluff structure situated on the Missionary Plain 160 kilometres west of Alice

Left: Group of three (of thirteen) meteorite impact craters at Henbury, south of Alice Springs in the Northern Territory. The largest crater is 180 metres in diameter. Thousands of fragments of iron meteorite have been found in the vicinity of the craters *(photo MJ Freeman)*.

Springs in the Northern Territory. One of the obvious differences between Wolfe Creek Crater and the Shoemaker structure, apart from their size, is the presence of an inner ring (now occupied by a lake) in the latter and a centrally uplifted area. Structures like Shoemaker and Gosses Bluff are called 'complex' structures and testify to truly catastrophic events in the geological past. Larger complex structures are sometimes 'multi-ringed'. These large structures are also sometimes called 'astroblemes'.

During the formation of large astroblemes, as with simple craters, the impacting projectile excavates a cavity by displacing, melting and vaporising the country rocks. However, the recoil of the rock beneath the point of impact lifts the cavity floor

Upturned strata and a rim raised above the surrounding country, splendidly shown by Wolfe Creek Crater, are characteristic features of meteorite explosion craters.

(Photo Dainis Dravins, Lund Observatory, Sweden)

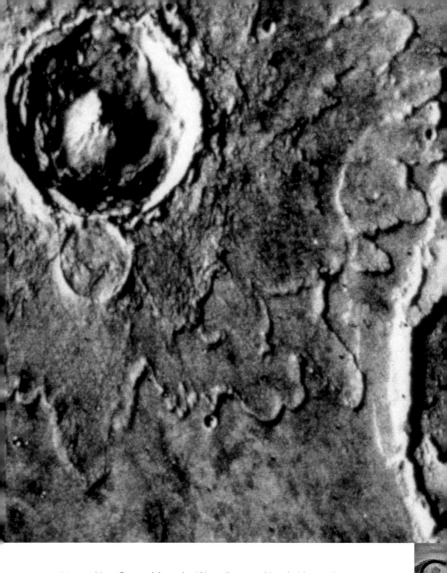

Above: Yuty Crater, Mars. At 19km diameter Yuty is bigger than Yallalie (13km), but it´s what Yallalie (see page 61) might have looked like when it formed *(photo NASA / http://www.lpi.usra.edu).*

upwards. The rim of the cavity collapses to form the final crater, which has a marked, centrally uplifted area surrounded by an annular depression. This depression is filled with brecciated and pulverised rock, and pools of impact-melted rock.

Shoemaker has been dated at around 600 million years old, while Gosses Bluff was formed about 142 million years ago. In that time the structures have been deeply eroded and only the lower levels, well below the original craters, are now preserved. This presents us with our first real problem, for in the absence of meteorites as proof of their origin what other than the circularity of such structures leads us to believe they were formed by impact?

Right: Goat Paddock (photo *NASA / http://www.lpi.usra.edu*).

Why Formed by a Meteorite?

There are thousands of circular structures on Earth's land surface, and many of these can be explained by the action of well-understood geological processes such as volcanism. A number of these structures do not occur in volcanic terrains, nor are they associated with volcanic material. Their origin is clearly enigmatic and in the past some scientists have described them as 'cryptovolcanic' or 'cryptoexplosion' structures, suggesting that they are the result of explosive eruptive activity or that the cause of the explosion is unknown. The main argument against this point of view is that many of these structures occur in very stable areas of Earth's crust where there has been no record of volcanic activity for many hundreds, perhaps thousands of millions of years. What, then, are the main features of some of these circular structures, apart from their shape, that lead us to believe they were formed by meteorite impact?

The telltale evidence of a meteoritic origin for structures like Shoemaker, Gosses Bluff, Lake Acraman and others falls into three main categories: structural, mineralogical and chemical. Geophysical surveys of many suspected impact structures show that they do not have deep-seated roots. For example, Gosses Bluff has a limit to the depth of severely disrupted rocks at around four kilometres below the present surface, indicating that the cause of the disruption could not have come from below, as in volcanic eruptions. However, the vital piece of evidence that distinguishes impact craters

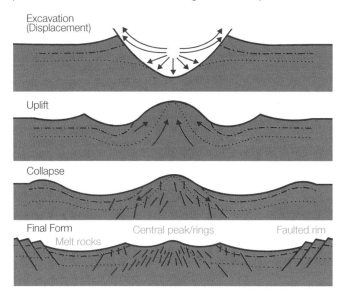

Excavation
(Displacement)

Uplift

Collapse

Final Form   Central peak/rings   Faulted rim
Melt rocks

Above: Stages in the formation of complex ringed structures such as Shoemaker (after Grieve, 1987).

from other geological formations is the presence of shock-altered minerals. The transient high pressures generated by the shock waves that excavate large craters cause transformations on a microscopic scale to occur in certain minerals in the target rocks. The diagnostic features of true impact structures include multiple sets of microscopic planar deformation features in quartz, a mineral that in its unaltered form has no natural cleavage. Significantly, impact cratering is the only geological process known to produce these so-called 'shock-metamorphic' effects abundantly. Other features include impact glasses (melted and rapidly solidified rock), and the rare minerals stishovite and coesite, which were formed by the intense compression of the mineral quartz.

The telltale evidence of a meteoritic origin for ancient, deeply eroded impact structures is threefold: structural, mineralogical and chemical.

In some impact structures like Popigai in Russia and the Nördlinger Ries structure in Germany, the country rocks are shot with tiny diamonds formed

Above: Shocked grain of quartz from the Woodleigh impact structure displaying multiple sets of closely spaced planar deformation features (field of view about four millimetres). Such deformation is caused by intense, short-lived shock waves that are characteristic of impact cratering, and are virtually unknown by any other geological process *(photo RM Hough)*.

by the shock-compression of graphite (carbon); some of these diamonds may even have condensed from the vapour generated by the impact. Since they survive over great periods of geological time, impact diamonds are additional useful indicators in the identification of impact structures. Recently, tiny diamonds of impact origin have been recognised within impact glass at the Henbury craters.

On a larger scale, other diagnostic features of

Above: Shatter cone, evidence of intense shock deformation in late Devonian sandstone from Gosses Bluff in the Northern Territory; width twenty centimetres *(photo K Brimmell).*

intensely shocked rocks are shatter cones, which are produced by the sliding of rocks along cone-shaped fractures. Like accusing fingers, the apices of the cones always point towards the point of impact. Shatter cones have not been found at Wolfe Creek Crater, but it is likely that erosion has not yet penetrated deeply enough to expose the shatter cones that may lie beneath the crater.

Evidence of giant impacts occasionally presents itself in places other than at the site of the collision. Rocks thrown great distances from craters that land in alien terrain, and flying glass such as tektite (far from the crater) or impactite (close to the crater), remain as incriminating evidence of impacts. Asteroids hitting seas and oceans raise giant tidal waves hundreds of metres high that break on land, depositing muddy sediments and other debris as they flow and ebb across hundreds of kilometres. Ejecta in the form of breccias are either hurled, or flow considerable distances from the crater from which they were ejected. In Australia, one of the best examples of the latter is seen at Yallalie in Western Australia.

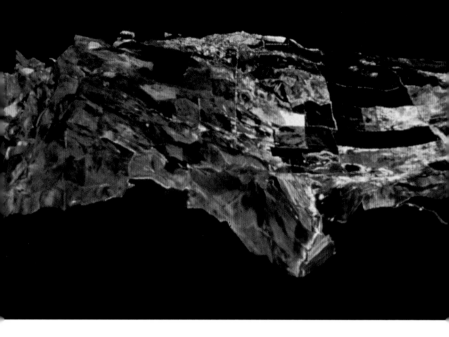

Pseudotachylite is an unusual kind of impact breccia that occurs deep in the target rocks of some large impact structures. In composition, pseudotachylites correspond closely to their adjacent host rocks, indicating that they formed from them by grinding, and sometimes frictional melting. Pseudotachylites can occur as thin, millimetre-sized veins, or bodies up to many tens of metres thick. They can contain numerous large and small rounded inclusions of milled target rock, set in a dense matrix that is generally black to blackish-green in colour.

Pseudotachylite-like rocks are not exclusive to

impact structures but also occur in zones of intense deformation, such as faults. They can result from sharp tectonic movements. Bodies of tectonic pseudotachylite tend to be linear and less than a few metres thick, whereas impact-produced pseudotachylites can form large, more irregular bodies developed over wide areas. Pseudotachylites then, are themselves not necessarily diagnostic of impacts unless they are accompanied by other evidence of shock-metamorphism. When pseudotachylites are present in impact structures,

factf⊙cus

Without meteorites as proof of an impact origin, the diagnostic indicators of impact are intensely shock-altered minerals in the crater rocks. On a microscopic scale, grains of quartz with multiple sets of planar deformation features confirm an impact origin.

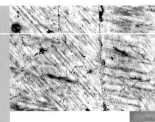

the melt-rich varieties offer a means of absolute age dating of the impact event.

Finally, in many impact craters gas from the vaporised projectile can be injected into the target rocks, leaving a distinctive chemical signature. The nature of the signature depends on the make-up of the meteoritic culprit, and it has been possible in some cases to identify the type of impacting meteorite from analysis of the melted rocks that make up the impact structure.

An example of telltale signs of a giant impact occurring in a place other than the impact site is the recognition of the Lake Acraman structure in the Gawler Ranges of South Australia as a huge

Other diagnostic features of impact cratering include shatter cones which are produced by the sliding of rocks along cone-shaped fractures. Shatter cones can vary in size from a few centimeters to many metres across.

Above: Magnetic image of the buried Yallalie structure (thirteen kilometres in diameter) reveals the central uplift and once highly terraced interior crater walls that are now marked by high magnetic responses *(photo P Hawke)*.

astrobleme. In 1983, geologists including Vic Gostin working in the Flinders Ranges some 300 kilometres east of Lake Acraman discovered a layer of shattered volcanic rock fragments, some up to thirty centimetres across, encased in 600-million-year-old shales in the Pichi Richi Pass, and in the same bed at other localities throughout the ranges.

Above: Breccia (sample twenty centimetres across) from the Yallalie impact structure in Western Australia. This mixture of rocks was formed from material ejected as a high-speed, turbulent, ground-hugging flow during the formation of the crater. Remnants of this breccia flow occur some four kilometres to the SW of the structure. It is now preserved as a distinct layer below subsequent sediments.

Dating of the foreign rocks in the layer showed that they were around 1000 million years older than the shales in which they had become embedded. Recognising that the rock fragments were typical of ancient volcanic rocks to be found at the Gawler Ranges, near Lake Acraman, the geologists deduced that they must have come from there — but how? Independently, in 1979, another geologist, George

Williams, had discovered abundant evidence of shocked mineral grains and shatter cones in the volcanic rocks exposed on the shores of the nearly circular Lake Acraman and concluded that it was an impact structure. Eventually, the geologists compared notes and realised that the rock fragments found in the Flinders Ranges represented some of the debris hurled from the impact at Lake Acraman. The estimated age of the host shales pinned down the time of the impact to around 600 million years ago.

At the time of the Lake Acraman impact, a shallow sea existed in the area now occupied by the Flinders Ranges. Debris from the impact rained down on the sea and sank into the muddy seabed, which later became buried by other sediments. Subsequent upheavals raised and contorted the accumulated sediments that now form the Flinders Ranges, and erosion has exposed the 'fossilised' remains of the fallout from the Acraman impact.

The original crater at Lake Acraman, which formed some 1–2 kilometres above the present land surface, was at least thirty kilometres in diameter, but circular fractures surrounding the impact site indicate that the final collapse crater could have been as much as 40–90 kilometres in diameter. This makes it one of the ten largest impact structures known in the world, and the energy released during its formation was around a million times greater than at Wolfe Creek Crater.

At impact angles between fifteen and ninety degrees, projectiles create circular, or nearly circular, craters. Below impact angles of fifteen degrees, craters take on an elongated shape. In Australia, several recently recognised elongate, basin-like structures have been suggested as possibly the result of low-angle impacts. The Flaxman (34°37'S, 139°04'E) and Crawford (34°43'S, 139°02'E) structures in South Australia, which may be related to a single event, are marked by telltale grains of shocked quartz and melted material. Other low-angle impacts include the Spider Structure in Western Australia, and Matt Wilson in the Northern Territory.

To date in Australia, thirty structures of various sizes have been identified to varying degrees of certainty as impact craters, or astroblemes. Another seven structures (making thirty-seven) have been recognised, but to date lack conclusive evidence of an origin by impact. Another twelve possible structures currently under investigation are not included in this total. Of those structures listed, fourteen occur in Western Australia, twelve in the Northern Territory, four in Queensland, five in South Australia, one in Tasmania, and one (Cleanskin) structure straddles the Northern Territory/Queensland border. The structures range in age from a few thousand years old, such as Dalgaranga crater in Western Australia, to more than a billion years old, such as Yarrabubba, also in Western Australia. Seventeen impact structures are dated at less than 200 million years old. This tendency towards 'younger'

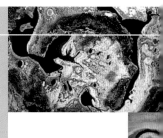

factf(ocu)s

Australian impact structures range in diameter from tens of metres to many tens of kilometres, and in age from a few thousand years to more than a billion years.

structures is consistent with evidence from other parts of the world and is due to the destruction of many older craters by prolonged weathering and erosion. Nevertheless, Australia has one of the best-preserved impact records in the world, dating back more than 500 million years.

The numbers of suspected impact craters known in Australia has varied from time to time without the recognition of new structures. For example, Fiery Creek Dome in Queensland and Spear Creek in the Northern Territory, long thought of as possible impact structures, are now discredited through lack of evidence. Accumulating undisputed, definitive evidence of impact is the most important aspect of crater studies. Only by establishing the impact origin of structures beyond doubt, and determining their sizes and ages accurately, can the data be used to calculate meaningful cratering rates through geological time, and predict the likelihood of another event occurring in future.

Above: Gosses Bluff, Northern Territory, viewed from space *(photo Australian Centre for Remote Sensing).*

Target Earth

Above: Looking into the bowl of Meteor (Barringer) Crater in Arizona, USA *(photo ©iStockphoto.com/StephanHoerold).*

In recent years, as a result of satellite photography and extensive geophysical exploration close to two hundred circular structures that may have been formed by giant meteorite impact have been recognised on Earth's surface and beneath the oceans. Many circular features, some up to one hundred kilometres or more in diameter, have been observed as ghostly outlines in some of the oldest rocks on Earth. Like Australia, other ancient continental landscapes such as the Canadian Shield, South Africa, Siberia and the Scandinavian Shield display faint circular scars that testify to the impact of huge asteroids millions of years ago. There is also gathering evidence that asteroidal impact may have, at various times, influenced geological and biological history. Locked away in ancient sediments on Earth are tantalising clues that at least one giant impact

may have caused a global holocaust.

The challenge of this particular 'crime' is that it happened 65 million years ago. Some scientists have argued that the victims may have been a large number of creatures, including the dinosaurs, which died out around that time. The evidence lies in a thin layer of clay that was deposited at the end of the geological period known as the Cretaceous. This clay, which marks the boundary between the Cretaceous and the succeeding Tertiary geological period, is unusually rich in the metal iridium. Of Earth's total budget of iridium, little remains in the crust. Along with other more abundant metallic elements, such as iron and nickel, most iridium sank to form Earth's metallic core very early in our planet's history. So where did the iridium in the clay layer come from?

The most likely sources are intense volcanic

eruptions or giant impact. Since meteorites contain more iridium than Earth's crust, the 'impact' hypothesis has gained many supporters in recent years. It has been suggested that a huge asteroid or comet about ten kilometres in diameter collided with Earth. The explosive power of such an impact would be greater than all the nuclear weapons currently held in the world's arsenals. If such a projectile struck the land surface, the body would punch a hole in Earth's crust, lifting more than 10,000 cubic kilometres of dust into the atmosphere. If the projectile plunged into an ocean, the giant wall of displaced water would flood the coastlines of most continents. Initially, Earth's surface would be plunged into freezing darkness. Without the life-

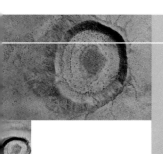

factf(ocu)s

Impact on the scale of Wolfe Creek Crater is predicted to occur perhaps once every 25,000 years. Potentially global catastrophic events, which might cause biological extinctions, may only occur on a time scale of 50-100 million years.

sustaining energy of the Sun, the food chain would be broken and large numbers of animals and plants would die. Later, the polluted atmosphere would cause a greenhouse effect and temperatures would rise dramatically. Gradually, as the dust settled, Earth would return to normal and the creatures and plants that survived could flourish once again.

In addition to iridium, the clay layer contains shock-altered minerals typical of meteorite impacts, and carbon residues indicating a global conflagration. The 'meteoritic' case for the exotic metals and other materials at the Cretaceous/Tertiary boundary has been argued strongly. Compelling physical evidence has tied the event to the huge Chicxulub structure (180 kilometres in diameter) on the Yucatan Peninsula in Mexico, but whether or not the impact was responsible for the extermination of the dinosaurs and other forms of life at that time is hotly disputed, and many palaeontologists are highly sceptical.

Although the dinosaurs dominated life on Earth for 140 million years, towards the end of the

Following Page: Alignment of the planets above Wolfe Creek Crater (photo John Goldsmith / Celestial Visions).

After Meteor Crater, Wolfe Creek Crater is the second largest authenticated meteorite crater associated with meteorites on land.

Above: Boundary between the Cretaceous and Tertiary geological periods (arrowed) at Stevns Klint, forty kilometres south of Copenhagen, Denmark. Clay at the boundary carries evidence of a global catastrophe 65 million years ago *(photo CL Smith)*.

Cretaceous their numbers had dwindled to about a dozen isolated species, and it would have taken very little to wipe them out completely. Curiously, other reptiles like the crocodiles and lizards, and many other groups of animals, such as the frogs, do not seem to have been affected by whatever caused the extinction of the dinosaurs. Many palaeontologists suggest that one specialised branch of the dinosaurs survives today as the birds. There is also much evidence from the geological record that the half-million years before the end of the Cretaceous was a period of severe environmental stress, with major, rapid fluctuations in global temperatures. In the case of marine microfossils, it has been found that it was only the rare, highly specialised forms that became extinct. But whatever the cause, it was very selective in which organisms did or did not become extinct. However, the disappearance of the dinosaurs at the end of the Cretaceous probably opened the way for another group of creatures: the mammals. And from that early stock, human beings evolved some 63 million years later.

A blast from the past

Just as happened at Chicxulub 65 million years ago, imagine an asteroid ten kilometres in diameter on a collision course with Earth. The average speed of such an encounter would be around thirty kilometres per second. Incredible as it may seem, initially the impact of such an object would tear a gaping hole twenty kilometres deep and eighty kilometres wide in Earth's crust. Momentarily, the projectile itself would continue to penetrate Earth at a few kilometres per second. Friction between the mountainous asteroid and the local rocks would generate a vast quantity of melt, some of which would be sprayed out the back of the brightly gaping hole.

Almost instantaneously the projectile would be flattened and stopped, and all its energy of movement converted to heat. A large proportion of the country rocks and projectile itself would melt and vaporise.

Shock waves generated by the impact would rebound from depth, lifting the floor of the cavity towards the surface. Like a huge beast coming up for air, the central uplift would burst through a sea of melt. Meanwhile, shock waves would propagate the crater outwards in every direction through landslides, eventually reaching its full diameter of around 180 kilometres. Tens of thousands of tonnes of dust would be hoisted into the air, blotting out the Sun and breaking the food chain. Initially, there would be freezing darkness. Acid rain would pollute the land. Later a greenhouse effect would raise temperatures dramatically. Gradually, as the dust settled, the atmosphere would cool, eventually allowing animals and plants to flourish once again. From the devastating impact of a ten-kilometre body to the final restoration of Earth's natural climatic systems would take around a million years.

Right: Wolfe Creek Crater *(photo Dainis Dravins, Lund Observatory, Sweden)*.

Can It
Happen Again?

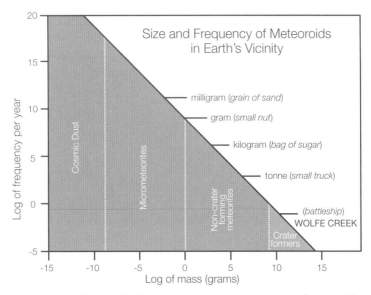

Above: Relationship between size and number of meteoroids near Earth. Because of the enormous ranges in both components, logarithmic scales are used. For example, on the horizontal scale of mass 0 = 1 gram, 5 = 100,000 grams and 10 = ten thousand million grams. Similarly on the vertical scale 5 = 100,000 whereas –5 = one hundred-thousandth or 1/100,000 (after Dodd, 1986).

Studies of bright meteors tell us that small meteorites, ranging from dust particles to objects much less than 100 grams, are far more abundant than large ones. How often, then, do potentially destructive bodies strike Earth? Crater-forming meteoroids — those weighing a few hundred tonnes or more — would be expected to strike Earth's land surface every twenty years or so. Theoretically, a meteoroid big enough to produce a crater the size of Wolfe Creek Crater, tens of thousands of tonnes, should arrive on Earth about once every 5000 years. However, a crater-forming impact on this scale has not occurred in historical times. The reason is that Earth is not without its natural defences, and there are a number of factors that work in our favour. Since three-quarters of Earth's surface is covered by water, most meteorites fall into the sea. Also, most meteorites are brittle objects and break up in the

Above: Old woodcut showing an imaginative fall of meteorites.

atmosphere to fall as many small objects rather than one large one. Studies of craters show that many were made by the impact of iron meteorites, which are far less common than stony meteorites and less prone to break-up in the atmosphere.

When all the mitigating factors are taken into account, impact-producing structures on the scale of Wolfe Creek Crater are predicted to occur perhaps once every 25,000 years, while collisions on the Lake Acraman and Gosses Bluff scale only about once every 15 million years or so. Potentially catastrophic global events like the Chicxulub impact, which might cause biological extinctions, may only occur on a time scale of 50–100 million years.

Realistically, what are the chances of catastrophic impact on Earth? If the fossil-cratering record is anything to go by, over the vast time-scale of geological history catastrophic impacts have certainly occurred and are indeed likely to occur again in the future. Humanity's written history is very short, a few thousand years or so, and this pales into insignificance against the 4,600 million years of Earth's geological history. Although unlikely, because large-scale cratering has not occurred during historical times, this does not mean it will not happen in the future. It is a sobering thought to know that astronomers predict there are more than two thousand asteroids greater than one kilometre in diameter in Earth-crossing orbit!

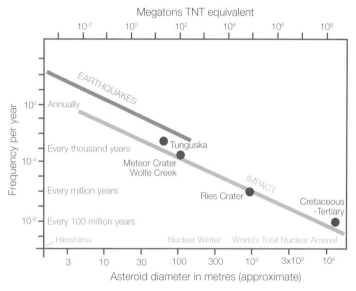

Above: Asteroid impact events with particular sizes related to energies in megatons of high explosive. Comparable Earth events, such as earthquakes and an atomic blast, and specific impact events (ground and atmospheric) are also shown. Estimates of the scale of the world's nuclear arsenal and of events required to induce a nuclear winter are indicated (after Grieve, 1998; Chapman and Morrison, 1994). It is estimated that there is a 1:30,000 chance of a major impact in the next century.

Australia's Impact Record (see map page 45 for locations)

CRATER	STATE	DIAMETER (km)	AGE (M.Y.)	EVIDENCE
AMELIA CREEK	NT	20x12	1640-600	Shatter cones, impact breccias
BOXHOLE	NT	0.17	0.0054 ± 0.0015	Meteorites
*CAMOOWEAL**	QLD	30	?	Buried structure, geophysics
CLEANSKIN STRUCTURE	NT/QLD	15	<1500	Shatter cones, shocked minerals
CONNOLLY BASIN	WA	9	60 ± 40	Shock features
CRAWFORD	SA	8.5x3.5	?	Elongated basin, shocked quartz
DARWIN CRATER	TAS	1.2	0.8 ± 0.04	Ejected glass impactites
DALGARANGA	WA	0.024	<0.003 (?)	Meteorites
FLAXMAN	SA	10x1	?	Elongated basin, shocked quartz
FOELSCHE	NT	~6	>600	Shocked quartz
GLIKSON	WA	~19	<508	Shocked minerals, shatter cones, geophysical anomaly
GOAT PADDOCK	WA	5	~55	Impactite melt breccia, shocked minerals, shatter cones
GOSSES BLUFF	NT	24	142.5 ± 0.8	Impact melts, shatter cones, shocked quartz
GOYDER	NT	9-12	<1400	Shocked quartz, shatter cones
*GUPULIYUL**	NT	8.5	1600-1325	Circular feature
HENBURY (Craters)	NT	0.18 (largest)	0.0042 ± 0.0019	Meteorites, impact glass
HICKMAN	WA	0.260	>0.01	Circular surface structure, deformation features
KELLY WEST	NT	10 - 20	>550	Shatter cones, shocked minerals
LAKE ACRAMAN	SA	>35	~580	Siderophiles, ejecta, melts, shatter cones, shocked minerals

*Those circular structures currently lacking conclusive evidence of an impact origin, or are otherwise considered doubtful, are in italics.

CRATER	STATE	DIAMETER (km)	AGE (M.Y.)	EVIDENCE
LAWN HILL	QLD	~18	>540	Impact melts, shatter cones, shocked minerals
LIVERPOOL CRATER	NT	1.6	140 (?)	Breccias, shock features, shocked minerals
MATT WILSON	NT	7.5x6.3	?	Disturbed rocks, shocked minerals
MT. TOONDINA	SA	3-4	<100 (?)	Shatter cones (?)
*MULKARRA**	SA	17-20	105±3	Buried structure, geophysics
PICCANINNY	WA	7	<360	Deformed rocks
SHOEMAKER (formerly Teague Ring)	WA	30	568±20 (?)	Shatter cones
SNELLING	WA	0.029x0.022	<0.005	Circular feature, breccias, shock features
SPIDER STRUCTURE	WA	11 x 13	>700	Shatter cones, shocked minerals
*SPRING RANGE**	NT	0.3	?	Geological feature
STRANGWAYS CRATER	NT	25-40	642±46	Siderophiles, shatter cones, impact melts, shocked minerals
*TALUNDILLY**	QLD	30	112-115	Buried structure, geophysics
TOOKOONOOKA	QLD	50 (?)	112-115	Buried structure, geophysics, shocked minerals
VEEVERS	WA	0.07	<0.004 (?)	Meteorites
WOLFE CREEK CRATER	WA	0.88	~0.34	Meteorites, shocked minerals, impact glass
WOODLEIGH	WA	60-70	359±4 (?)	Buried structure, geophysics, shocked quartz
YALLALIE	WA	13	>65	Buried structure, geophysics, breccias
YARRABUBBA	WA	>30	>1134±26 (?)	Shocked quartz, impact melts, shatter cones

83

Glossary

Asteroids

Small planet-like bodies (or large fragments thereof) that orbit the Sun, mostly occupying the region between Mars and Jupiter.

Bed

A recognisable unit of rock, such as a layer of sandstone or shale, which has a top and a bottom defined by junction with layers of rock above and below of slightly different consistency.

Cleavage

The tendency for crystals of many minerals to split along certain definite planes — the cleavage-planes — that are closely related to the crystalline form and internal atomic structure of each mineral.

Comet

Body formed of ice and rock that comes from the extreme regions of the Solar System. Comets become visible when their orbits change, bringing them into the inner Solar System where heating from the Sun causes their ices to vaporise and form a 'coma', releasing gas and dust into tails. Cometary tails always point away from the Sun.

Cretaceous

Period of geological time (and corresponding system of rocks) between 145 and 65 million years ago. It is named after the Latin word for chalk (creta) because of chalk beds of this age. The last known dinosaur fossils occur in rocks of latest Cretaceous age.

Devonian

Period of geological time (and corresponding system of rocks) between about 415 and 360 million years ago. Named after Devon, a county in England where rocks of this age were first studied. Known as the 'age of fishes', the Devonian marked a peak of diversity for the first fishes.

Gypsum

Hydrated calcium sulphate ($CaSO_4.2H_2O$). This mineral may occur as large crystals of selenite, finely crystalline alabaster, or fibrous satin spar. It occurs commonly in mud and shale in Australia in ephemeral lakes.

Iron meteorite

Meteorite made mainly of iron-nickel metal.

Laterite

A weathering product formed in wet tropical regions as a result of the decomposition of rock. It consists predominantly of iron and aluminium oxides. It often forms a hard, brown surface layer.

Meteoroid

An extraterrestrial body in space.

Meteor

Transient light phenomenon caused by the melting and vaporisation of a small object on entry into the upper atmosphere. Also called 'shooting stars', meteors are bright moving lights that leave luminous trails.

Meteorite

A natural object that survives its fall to Earth from space. There are three basic types: iron, stony-iron and stony meteorites. Stones are the most common types seen to fall.

Mineral

Naturally occurring substance with a definite chemical composition and regular, crystalline internal arrangement of atoms.

Precambrian

The name of the period of Earth's history from its inception some 4,550 million years ago up to about 542 million years ago, at which time there was a great evolutionary explosion of life forms in the seas. They also developed hard shells and so were easily fossilised.

Quarzite

A quartz-rich (silicon dioxide, SiO_2) sandstone. The term is often used for sandstones that have been recrystallised by heat and pressure.

Shales

Fine-grained, laminated sedimentary rocks formed by the compression of clay, silt or mud.

Shatter cones

Cone-like, striated fractures in rocks subjected to high shock pressures.

Sink holes

Fissures formed at Earth's surface by cracking or erosion of areas of weakness; subterranean subsidence may also occur.

Tektite

Naturally occurring once-airborne glass ejected by explosive meteorite impact in the geological past.

Tertiary

Period of geological time (and corresponding system of rocks) from about 65 to 1.8 million years ago immediately following the Cretaceous.

Sources and Selected Further Reading

Alvarez, LW, Alvarez, W, Asaro, F and Michel, HV (1980). 'Extraterrestrial cause for the Cretaceous-Tertiary extinction.' *Science*, 208:1095–1108.

Artemieva, N (2002). 'Tektite Origin in Oblique Impacts: Numerical Modelling of the Initial Stage.' In Plado, J and Pesonen, LJ (eds). *Impacts in Precambrian Shields*. Springer-Verlag, pp 257–276.

Bevan, AWR and de Laeter, JR (2002). *Meteorites: A Journey through Space and Time*. University of New South Wales Press, pp 215.

Bevan, AWR and Hough, RM (2002). 'Blasts from the Past: Age and Size Do Matter.' *Geoscientist*, 12(2):4–7.

Bland, PA, de Souza Filho, CR, Jull, AJT, Kelley, SP, Hough, RM, Artemieva, NA, Pierazzo, E, Coniglio, J, Pinotti, L, Evers, V and Kearsley, AT (2002). 'A possible tektite strewn field in the Argentinian Pampa.' *Science*, 296:1109–1111.

Buffetaut, E and Koeberl, C (eds) (2002). *Geological and Biological Effects of Impact Events*. Springer-Verlag, Berlin Heidelberg, 295 pp.

Cassidy, WA (1954). 'The Wolf Creek, Western Australia, meteorite crater.' *Meteoritics*, 1:197–199.

Chapman, CR and Morrison, D (1994). 'Impacts on Earth by asteroids and comets: Assessing the hazard.' *Nature*, 367, pp 33–34.

Dentith, MC, Bevan, AWR, Backhouse, J, Featherstone, WE and Koeberl, C (1999). 'Yallalie: A buried structure of possible impact origin in the Perth Basin, Western Australia.' *Geological Magazine*, 136:619–632.

Dietz, RS (1959). 'Shatter cones in cryptoexplosion structures (meteorite impact?).' *Journal of Geology*, 67:496–505.

Dodd, RT (1986). *Thunderstones and Shooting Stars: The Meaning of Meteorites*. Harvard University Press, Cambridge, Massachusetts, 196 pp.

Dypvik, H, Burchell, M, and Claeys, P (eds) (2004). *Cratering in Marine Environments and on Ice*. Springer-Verlag, Berlin Heidelberg, 340 pp.

Faust, GT, Fahey, JF, Mason, BH and Dwornik, EJ (1973). 'The disintegration of the Wolf Creek meteorite and the formation of pecoraite, the nickel analog of clinochrysotile.' U. S. Geological Survey, Professional Paper 384-C:1–35.

French, BM (1998). *Traces of Catastrophe: A Handbook of Shock-Metamorphic Effects in Terrestrial Meteorite Impact Structures*. LPI Contribution No 954, Lunar and Planetary Institute, Houston, 120 pp.

Fudali, RF and Ford, R (1979). 'Darwin glass and Darwin Crater: a progress report.' *Meteoritics*, 14:283–296.

Glikson, AY (ed) (1996). 'Australian impact structures.' AGSO *Journal of Australian Geology and Geophysics*, 16, No 4, pp 371–587.

Glikson, AY, Hickman, AH and Vickers, J (2008). 'Hickman Crater, Opthalmia Range, Western Australia: Evidence supporting a meteorite impact origin.' *Australian Journal of Earth Sciences*, 55:1107–1117.

Gostin, VA, Haines, PW, Jenkins, RJF, Compston, W, and Williams, IS (1986). 'Impact ejecta horizon within Late Precambrian Shales, Adelaide Geosyncline, South Australia.' *Science*, 233:198–200.

Grady, MM, Hutchison, R, McCall, GJH and Rothery, DA (1998). *Meteorites: Flux with Time and Impact effects*. Geological Society, London, Special Publications, 140, 278 pp.

Grieve, RAF (1987). 'Terrestrial impact structures.' *Annual Review of Earth and Planetary Sciences*, 16:245–270.

Grieve, RAF (1990). 'Impact cratering on Earth.' *Scientific American*, 19(1):66–73.

Grieve, RAF (1991). 'Terrestrial impacts: The record in the rocks.' *Meteoritics*, 26:175–194.

Grieve, RAF (1998). *Extraterrestrial Impacts on Earth: The Evidence and the Consequences*. In Glikson, AY (ed) (1996). Australian Impact Structures. AGSO Journal of Australian Geology and Geophysics, 16, No 4, pp 371–587.

Guppy, JD and Matheson, RS (1950). 'Wolf Creek Crater, Western Australia.' *Journal of Geology*, 58:30–36.

Haines, PW (1989). 'Probable impact structure near Barrow Creek, Northern Territory.' *Australian Journal of Earth Sciences*, 36:135–137.

Haines, PW (1996). 'Goyder impact structure, Arnhem Land, Northern Territory.' *AGSO Journal of Australian Geology and Geophysics*, 16:561–566.

Haines, PW (2005). 'Impact cratering and distal ejecta: The Australian Record.' *Australian Journal of Earth Sciences*, 52:481–507.

Haines, PW and Rawlings, DJ (2002). 'The Foelsche structure, Northern Territory, Australia: An impact crater of probable Neoproterozoic age.' *Meteoritics and Planetary Science*, 37:269–280.

Haines, PW, Sweet, I and Mitchell, K (2008). 'The Cleanskin Structure: A preliminary report on a large impact structure in the Mesoproterozoic South Nicholson Group, Northern Australia.' Australian Earth Sciences Convention Perth, Western Australia (abstract) 127.

Haines, PW, Therriault, AM and Kelley, SP (1999). 'Evidence for Mid-Cenozoic (?), low-angle multiple impacts in South Australia.' *Meteoritics and Planetary Science*, 34:A49–50.

Hawke, PJ, Buckingham, AJ and Dentith, MC (2003). 'Origin of the magnetic anomalies associated with the Yallalie impact structure, Perth Basin, Western Australia.' ASEG 16th Geophysical Conference and Exhibition, Adelaide, Etended Abstracts.

Hildebrand, AR, Pilkington, M, Ortiz-Aleman, C, Chavez, RE,

Urrutia-Fucugauchi, J, Connors, M, Graniel-Castro, E, Camara-Zi, A, Halpenny, JF and Niehaus, D (1998). 'Mapping Chicxulub crater structure with gravity and seismic reflection data.' In: Grady, MM, Hutchison, R, McCall, GJ H and Rothery, DA (eds). *Meteorites: Flux with Time and Impact Effects*. Geological Society, London, Special Publications, 140:155–176.

Hodge, PW and Wright, FW (1971). 'Meteoritic particles in the soil surrounding the Henbury Meteorite Craters.' *Journal of Geophysical Research*, 76:3880–3895

Holmes, CH (1948). 'The hidden crater of Wolf Creek.' *Walkabout Magazine*, November edition:10–16.

Hough, RM, Gilmour, I, Pillinger, CT, Arden, JW, Gilkes, KWR, Yuan, J, and Milledge, HJ (1995). 'Diamond and silicon carbide in impact melt rock from the Ries impact crater.' *Nature*, 378:41–44.

Hough, RM, Lee, MR, and Bevan, AWR (2003). 'Characterisation and significance of shocked quartz from the Woodleigh impact structure, Western Australia.' *Meteoritics and Planetary Science*, 38:1341–1350.

Howard, KT (2008). 'Geochemistry of Darwin glass and target rocks from Darwin Crater, Tasmania, Australia.' *Meteoritics and Planetary Science*, 43:479–496.

Howard, KT and Haines, PW (2007). 'The geology of Darwin Crater, western Tasmania, Australia.' *Earth and Planetary Science Letters*, 260(1–2):328–339.

Kenkmann, T and Poelchau, MH (2008). 'Matt Wilson: An elliptical impact crater in Northern Territory, Australia.' Lunar and Planetary Science Conference XXXIX, Lunar and Planetary Institute, Houston (CD-ROM), Abstract #1027.pdf

Kenkmann, T and Poelchau, MH (2009). 'Low-angle collision with Earth: The elliptical impact crater Matt Wilson, Northern Territory, Australia.' *Geology*, 37:459–462.

Koeberl, C and Martinez-Ruiz, F (eds) (2003). Impact Markers in the Stratigraphic Record. Springer-Verlag, Berlin Heidelberg, 347 pp.

McCall, GJ H, (ed) (1977). 'Meteorite Craters.' *Benchmark Papers in Geology* 36, Dowden, Hutchison and Ross, Stroudsburg, Pennsylvania, 364 pp.

McCall, GJH (ed) (1979). 'Astroblemes: Cryptoexplosion structures.' *Benchmark Papers in Geology* 50, Dowden, Hutchison and Ross, Stroudsberg, Pennsylvania, 437 pp.

McCall, GJH (2001). Tektites in the Geological Record Showers of glass from the sky. *Geological Society of London*, 256 pp.

Macdonald, FA, Bunting, JA and Cina, SE (2003). 'Yarrabubba: A large, deeply eroded impact structure in the Yilgarn Craton, Western Australia.' *Earth and Planetary Science Letters*, 213:235–247, and erratum, (2004) 226:545.

Macdonald, FA, and Mitchell, K (2003). 'Amelia Creek, Northern Territory, Australia: A 20x12 km oblique impact structure with no central uplift.' Workshop on Impact Cratering. 8006. pdf.

McNamara, KJ and Bevan AWR (2001). *Tektites* 3rd (revised and enlarged) edition. Western Australian Museum, 38 pp.

MacLeod, N (1998). 'Impacts and marine invertebrate extinctions.' In: Grady, MM, Hutchison, R, McCall, GJH and Rothery, DA (eds). *Meteorites: Flux with Time and Impact Effects*. Geological Society, London, Special Publications, 140:217–246.

Melosh, HJ (1988). *Impact Cratering: A Geological Process*. Oxford University Press, 245 pp.

Milner, AC (1998). 'Timing and causes of vertebrate extinction across the Cretaceous–Tertiary boundary.' In: Grady, MM, Hutchison, R, McCall, GJH and Rothery, DA (eds). *Meteorites: Flux with Time and Impact Effects*. Geological Society, London, Special Publications, 140:247–257.

Milton, DJ, Barlow, BC, Brett, R, Brown, AR, Glikson, AY, Manwaring, EA, Moss, FJ, Sedmik, ECE, Van Son, J, and Young, GA (1972). 'Gosses Bluff impact structure, Australia.' *Science*, 175:119–1207.

Montanari, A and Koeberl, C (2000). *Impact Stratigraphy: The*

Italian Record. Springer — Berlin, Heidelberg, New York, Barcelona, Hong Kong, London, Milan, Paris, Singapore, Tokyo 364 pp.

Mory AJ, Iasky, RP, Glikson, AY and Pirajno, F (2000). 'Woodleigh, Carnarvon Basin, Western Australia: A new 120 km diameter impact structure.' *Earth and Planetary Science Letters*, 177:119–128.

Peuker-Ehrenbrink, B and Schmitz, B (eds) (2001). *Accretion of Extraterrestrial Matter throughout Earth's History.* New York, Kluwer Academic/Plenum, 466 pp.

Plescia, JB (1999) 'Mulkarra impact structure South Australia: A complex impact structure.' Lunar and Planetary Science Conference XXX, Lunar and Planetary Institute, Houston (CD-ROM), Abstract #1889.pdf.

Reeves, F and Chalmers, RO (1949). 'The Wolf Creek Crater.' *Australian Journal of Earth Science*, 11:154–156.

Reimold, WU, Koeberl, C, Hough, RM, McDonald, I, Bevan, A, Amare, K, and French, BM (2003). 'Woodleigh impact structure, Australia: Shock petrography and geochemical studies.' *Meteoritics and Planetary Science*, 38:1109–1130.

Roddy, DJ, Pepin, RO and Merrill, RB (eds) (1977). *Impact and Explosion Cratering.* Pergamon Press, 1301 pp.

Sharpton, VL and Wards, PD (eds) (1990). 'Global catastrophes in Earth history: An interdisciplinary conference on impacts, volcanism and mass mortality.' Geological Society of America Special Paper, 247, 631 pp.

Shoemaker, EM (1983). 'Asteroid and comet bombardment of the Earth.' *Annual Review of Earth and Planetary Sciences*, 11:461–494.

Shoemaker, EM, Macdonald, FA and Shoemaker, CS (2005). 'Geology of five small Australian impact craters.' *Australian Journal of Earth Sciences*, 52:529–544.

Shoemaker, EM and Shoemaker, CS (1988). 'Impact structures of Australia.' *Lunar and Planetary Science*, 19:1079–1080.

Shoemaker, EM and Shoemaker, CS (1997). 'Glikson, a probable impact structure, Western Australia.' *Lunar and Planetary Science*, 28, http://www.lpi.usra.edu/meetings/lpsc97/pdf/1669.PDF

Sweet, IP, Haines, PW and Mitchell, K (2005). 'Matt Wilson structure: Record of an impact event of possible early Mesoproterozoic age, Northern Territory, Australia.' *Australian Journal of Earth Sciences*, 52:675–688.

Taylor, SR (1965). 'The Wolf Creek iron meteorite.' *Nature*, 208:944–945.

Taylor, SR (2001). *Solar System Evolution: A New Perspective*, 2nd edition. Cambridge University Press, 460pp.

Thompson, RB (1991). *A Guide to the Geology and Landforms of Central Australia*. Alice Springs, Northern Territory Geological Survey, pp 31–32.

Tonkin, PC (1998). 'Lorne Basin, New South Wales: Evidence for a possible impact origin.' *Australian Journal of Earth Sciences*, 45:669–671.

White, JS, Henderson, EP and Mason, B (1967). 'Secondary minerals produced by weathering of Wolf Creek meteorite.' *American Mineralogist*, 52:1190–1197.

Williams, GE (1986). 'The Acraman impact structure: Source of Ejecta in Late Precambrian shales, South Australia.' *Science*, 233:200–203.

Yang, D and Veblen, DR (2004). 'Impactite from Henbury, Australia.' *American Mineralogist*, 89:961–968.

Yeates, AN, Crowe, RWA and Towner, RR (1976). 'The Veevers Crater: a possible meteoritic feature.' *BMR Journal of Australian Geology and Geophysics*, 1:77–78.

Websites

http://www.unb.ca/passc/ImpactDatabase/austr.html

http://whc.unesco.org/en/list/1162

Acknowledgements

The authors thank Peter Haines, Jennifer Bevan and Rob Hough for kindly reading an earlier version of the manuscript and offering helpful suggestions for its improvement. We are also grateful to Rob Hough for writing a foreword to this new and enlarged edition. Kris Brimmell, Russell Hudson, Geoff Deacon and Dainis Dravins are thanked for some of the photographic material. Peter Bindon is thanked for information on the Aboriginal legend. Mike Freeman and Tony Yeates are thanked for providing the photographs of the Henbury craters and Veevers crater, respectively, and Phil Hawke is thanked for providing the Yallalie magnetic image. The Department of Land Administration, Landgate (Perth), through Andrew Buchanan and Robert Shaw, and the Australian Centre for Remote Sensing (ACRES) are thanked for providing the digitally enhanced satellite images of Australian impact structures. Danielle West is thanked for drafting the figures.

First Published 2009 by the
Western Australian Museum
49 Kew Street, Welshpool, Western Australia 6106
(Postal: Locked Bag 49, Welshpool DC. WA 6986)
www.museum.wa.gov.au

Designer Cathie Glassby
Printed by South Wind Productions, Singapore.

National Library of Australia
Cataloguing-in-publication entry
Author: Bevan, Alex.
Title: Australia's meteorite craters / Alex Bevan, Ken
McNamara.
Edition: 2nd ed.
ISBN: 9781920843960 (pbk.)
Notes: Bibliography.
Subjects: Meteorite craters — Australia.
Other Authors/Contributors: I. McNamara, Ken.
II. Western Australian Museum.
Dewey Number: 551.3970994